Graphs Don't Lie

or

How to Lie with Graphs and Get Away With It...

Copyright

Graphs Don't Lie

By Lee Baker

Copyright 2018 Lee Baker

Amazon Paperback Edition

Thank you for purchasing this book. You are welcome to share it with your friends.

No part of this publication may be reproduced, copied, stored in a retrieval system or transmitted in any form or by any means without the prior written permission of the publisher

If you enjoyed this book, please return to your favourite book retailer to discover other works by this author.

Thank you for your support.

Contents

Introduction

Truncate the y-axis

Truncate the x-axis

Omit the y-axis labels

Extrapolate

Pie Charts

3D Charts

Pictocharts

Epilogue

About The Author

Claim Your Free eBook Now!

Leave a Review

Claim Your FREE eBook Now!

This is the sister book to **Graphs Don't Lie**, and teaches you how to lie with statistics

(if you're unscrupulous enough…)

Download your FREE copy right here:

https://chi2innovations.lpages.co/ebook-truth-lies-and-statistics/

Introduction

When I do something, I give it everything I've got. It's just the way I am and I don't think I'll ever change. And if you add up all of that 'everything', what do you get? 100%. You can't give more than that. Unless you're a footballer, where 110% is standard. But for the rest of us mere mortals, it's 100%.

Apparently, though, if you work for Fox News then 193% is the sum total of everything there is.

During the 2012 US primaries, Fox News presented a wonderful pie chart showing the support levels that all three candidates enjoyed. It was a very slick presentation with a nice, shiny 3D chart, and anchorman Bryon Harlan said that Sarah Palin currently has the most support for the 2012 presidential nomination among Republican candidates.

"When it comes to landing the nomination," said Harlan, quoting directly from the pie chart on the screen, "Palin is at 70%, about a third higher than this past July". Wow, 70% – it looks like she's running away with it. Surely, none of the other candidates could catch her now, not with such large levels of support.

"Mike Huckabee," he continued, "stands at 63%, with Mitt Romney at 60%". Wait, what? What just happened? The total support for all three candidates apparently stands at 193%. What does this mean? Does it mean that 193% of eligible voters will turn out in the primaries, or perhaps that this pie chart is 193% as effective as typical pie charts? No idea, but what I do know for sure is that there were some seriously under-handed shenanigans going on there.

You see, the thing about graphs is that they don't lie. You put some numbers into a spreadsheet, tell it which graph you want, and out pops a faithful representation of your data. If you give it the numbers 70, 63 and 60, it will plot them on your chosen graph, even as a pie chart. It won't change the numbers, give them political spin or otherwise misrepresent them. It doesn't know how to.

People, on the other hand, do.

Graphs might not lie, but if you plot biased data on a graph or elect to represent truthful data on an inappropriate graph, you'll be guilty of misleading your audience. And that's the whole point.

When plotting graphs and charts you have choices and some of the choices are more appropriate than others. Do you want to tell the truth? Then choose wisely. Would you like your company to make more money or your preferred candidate to garner more votes? Perhaps you might prefer to choose a little less wisely. If you're comfortable with using graphs to misrepresent the truth – and even prefer them as a vehicle for profit or career enhancement – then this book will help you find lots of ways to tell untruths with your graphs.

A word of caution though: this book was not written for you. It was written to help the conscientious spot when you're trying to pull the wool over their eyes. After all, the crooks and conmen already know these tricks, and it falls to honest men to learn them in self-defence.

Truncate the y-axis

Most graphs you'll come across are at least mostly truthful, but from time to time, you'll come across the odd one here and there that just makes your eyes pop out, like this one:

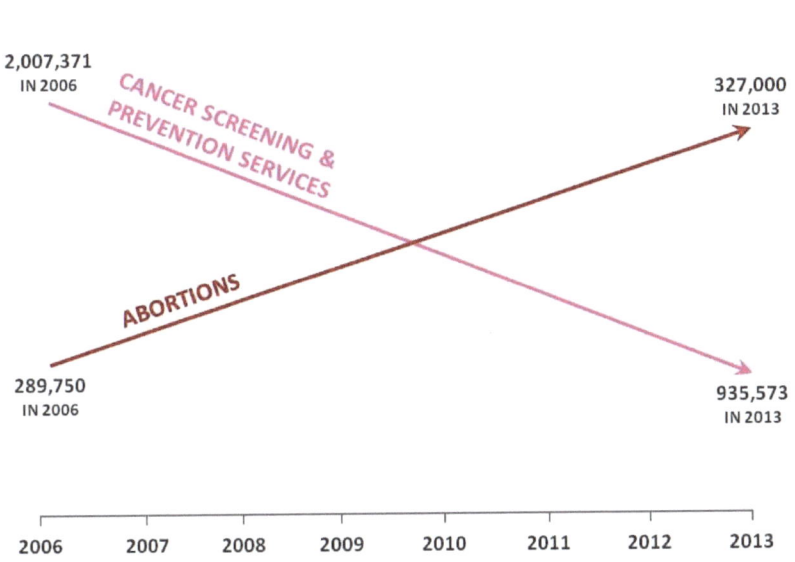

Referring to this graph in a 2015 Congressional hearing, Republican Jason Chaffetz said "In 2006, Planned Parenthood performed more prevention services and cancer screenings than abortions, but in 2013, there were more abortions".

"In pink," he continued, "that's the reduction in the breast exams, and the red is the increase in the abortions. That's what's going on in your organisation."

Oh my, where to start...

Firstly, the chart features a pair of lines crossing, one heading upwards (abortions) and the other heading downwards (cancer screening and prevention services). The data appear to show substantial growth in the number of abortions, coinciding with a visually comparable decrease in the number of cancer screenings. The numbers on the chart are based on real data and at first inspection, the facts appear damning – the implication from the graph is that there has been a switch in focus away from cancer towards more abortions. We need to look closer though, and in particular notice how the two lines are on completely different scales – the cancer data are plotted in the millions, while the abortion data are plotted in the hundreds of thousands. The number of cancer screening and prevention services in 2013 is lower on the graph than the number of abortions, and yet there are almost 3 times as many cancer interventions as abortions in that year. If you believe that this graph is correct, then you must also believe that 327,000 is a larger number than 935,573!

The creator of the graph put cancer on the primary y-axis, abortions on a secondary y-axis, truncated them both so that the lines cross in the middle, then omitted both y-axes to cover up the deception. In fact checking the graph, it was discovered that the chart came from Americans United for Life – an anti-abortion group – who insisted that the graphic was "accurate and honest". Sure it was! "That graphic is a damn lie," said Albert Cairo, a visual communications expert at the University of Miami, "regardless of whatever people think of this issue, this distortion is ethically wrong." Enrico Bertini, a professor at New York University who studies data visualisation called the chart "scandalous".

For balance, on the next page are the actual data when plotted on a single non-truncated y-axis.

These data don't look quite so damning, do they? You could hardly have come to the conclusion from this graph that there was a switch in focus from cancer to abortions – in fact, it appears that there is no increase in abortions at all. This is because of the difference in scales between the two plot lines – any change in the abortion data has to be large for it to show up on the graph.

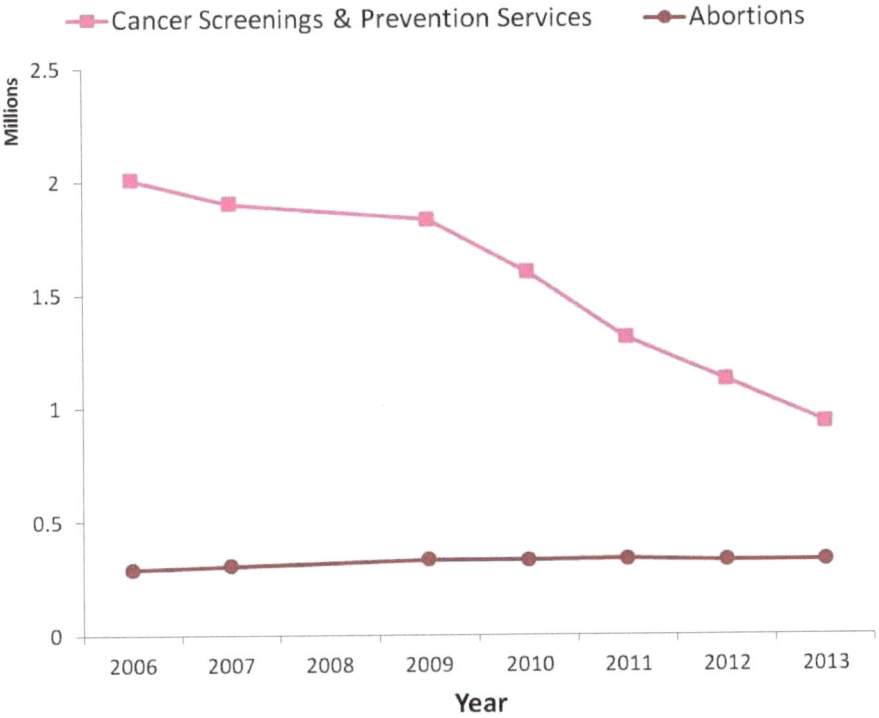

If you wanted to show the relative change of each of these two sets of data, you could plot the percentage change of each of the parameters from their 2006 baseline. Doing so would result in the graph overleaf.

From this plot, we can see that the number of abortions did increase by about 15% from 2006 to 2009. It is indeed *after* 2009 – when the abortion rate remained constant – that we see large decreases in cancer screenings and prevention services. It is clear from this graph that there is not a switch of focus from cancer to abortions, in direct contradiction to what the Americans United for Life graph appears to show.

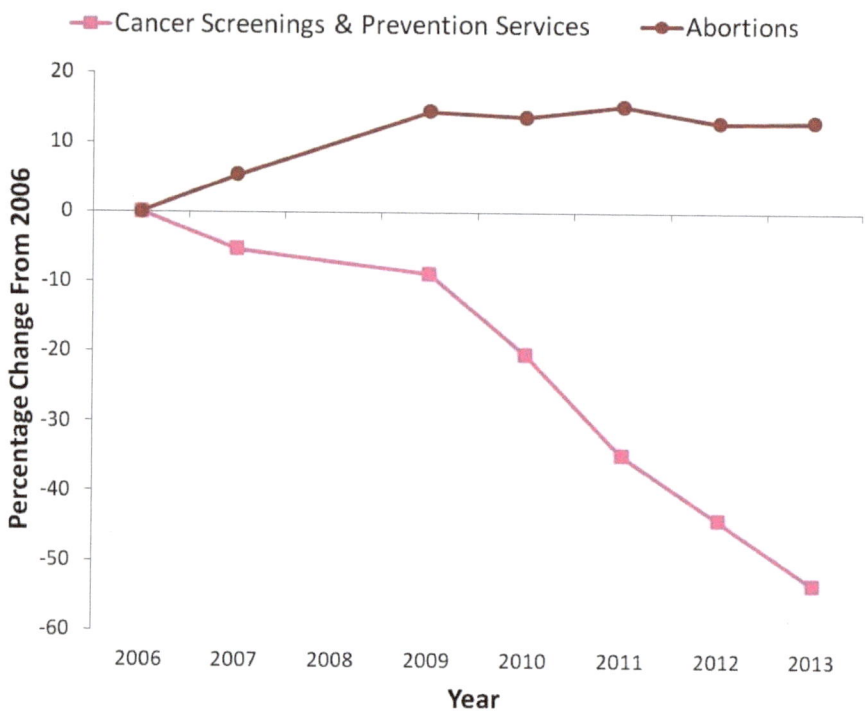

Why did the cancer screening rate drop after this year? In 2009, the US Preventative Services Task Force updated its recommendation to get mammogram screenings every two years instead of its previous suggestion of every 12 months.

Truncate the x-axis

A favoured way of misleading the reader is to show only the data you wish them to see. In statistical terms, this would be known as **selective reporting**, but we also do this in graphs by truncating the x-axis and showing only selective data that make your point.

At some point at the beginning of the 21st Century, there was a seismic shift in political opinion. Prior to this point politicians argued that the world was not warming, and even if it were, it would cost HUGE amounts of money to reverse. Then the shift happened. Politicians realised that rather than taking such costs out of government budgets they could make the people pay for it instead. Once they realised that climate change could even be *profitable*, global warming started to become something of a religion. Actually, it became two distinct religions – those in favour of the theory of anthropomorphic climate change (humans caused the planet to warm) and those against. Both sides have used precisely the same data to try to make their point.

There is one graph in particular that is used time and again by the naysayers to 'prove' that the planet is not warming, but is actually *cooling*.

Let's take a look at the data and see how they managed to come up with that conclusion. We start by taking the global mean temperature from 1880 to 2014 and graph it (overleaf).

It's not very informative – it seems to suggest that there has been no change in temperature over the past 100+ years. That's because the graph lacks context – the absolute temperature is unimportant, it is the *change* in temperature that is a cause for concern. Scientists generally agree that a change of only a few degrees would have catastrophic consequences for all life on earth, and that efforts should be made to limit global warming to less than 2.0°C (3.6°F) of pre-industrial levels.

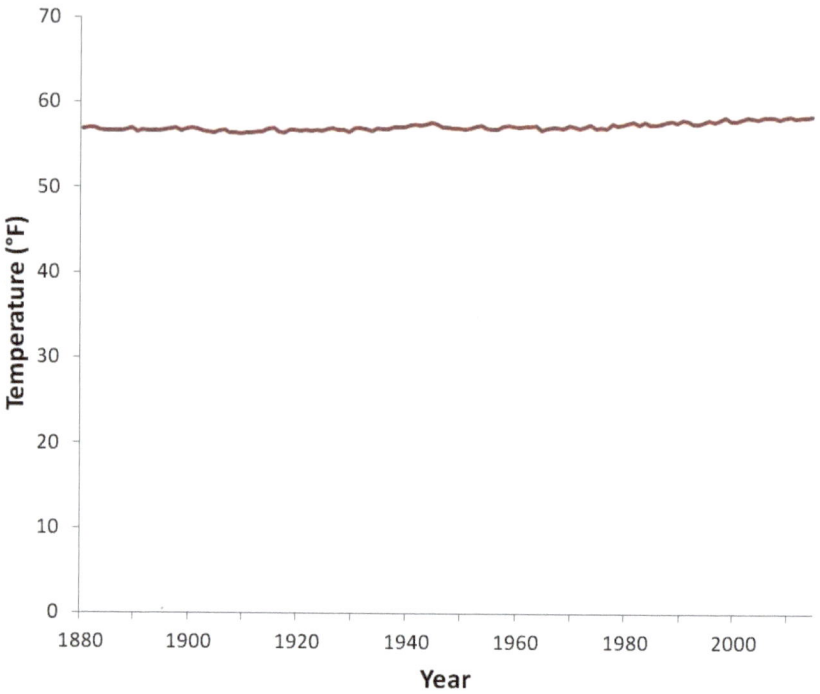

It makes sense, then, to calculate the change in temperature and plot that instead (overleaf).

That's better, much more detail. The data clearly show that there has been an increase in global temperature of around 1.7°F since 1880 and a rise of around 2.2°F between the lowest and highest recorded annual temperatures (56.35°F in 1909 to 58.53°F in 2014).

That is quite a substantial change, so it's pretty impossible to make these data show that the planet is cooling, isn't it? Au contraire!

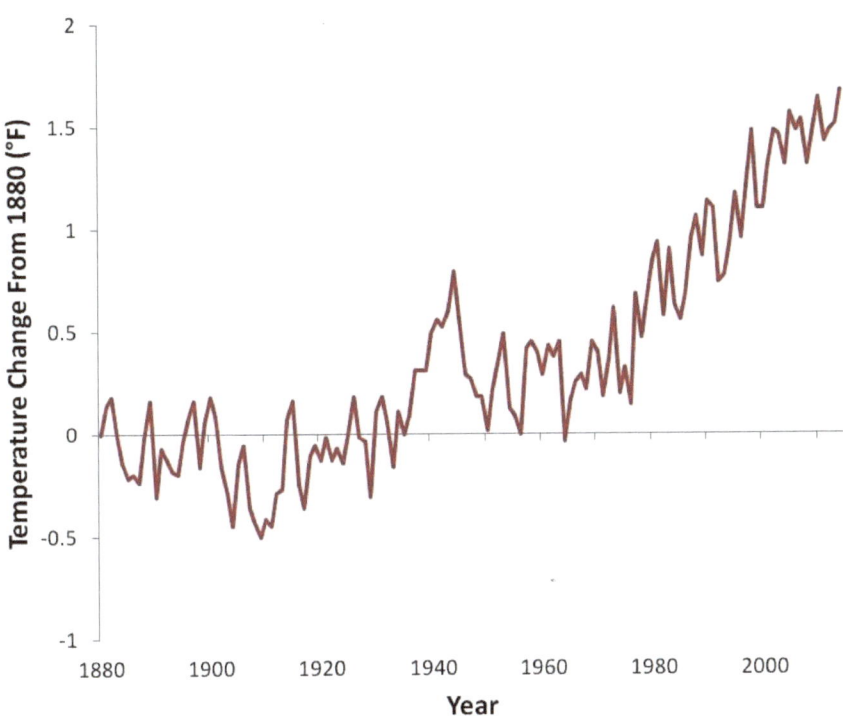

Using the simple trick of truncating the x-axis to highlight a specific range of temperatures while conveniently ignoring all other data will get us to where we need to be. Look at the region in the data between 1998 and 2011. This certainly *looks like* there could be some data in there that we can use to make a convincing argument, so let's plot that and see what it looks like (overleaf).

To aid the point we're trying to make I've changed the plot to black and added in a red arrow to accentuate the downward trend of the temperatures (as opposed to a best fit trend line, which would have an upward slope).

This graph is actually used by climate change deniers as their reference to disprove global warming. They argue that over this 13 year period there was a clear decrease in global temperatures, any warming in the planet has reached a plateau and there is no cause for alarm. Nothing to see here, move along, move along...

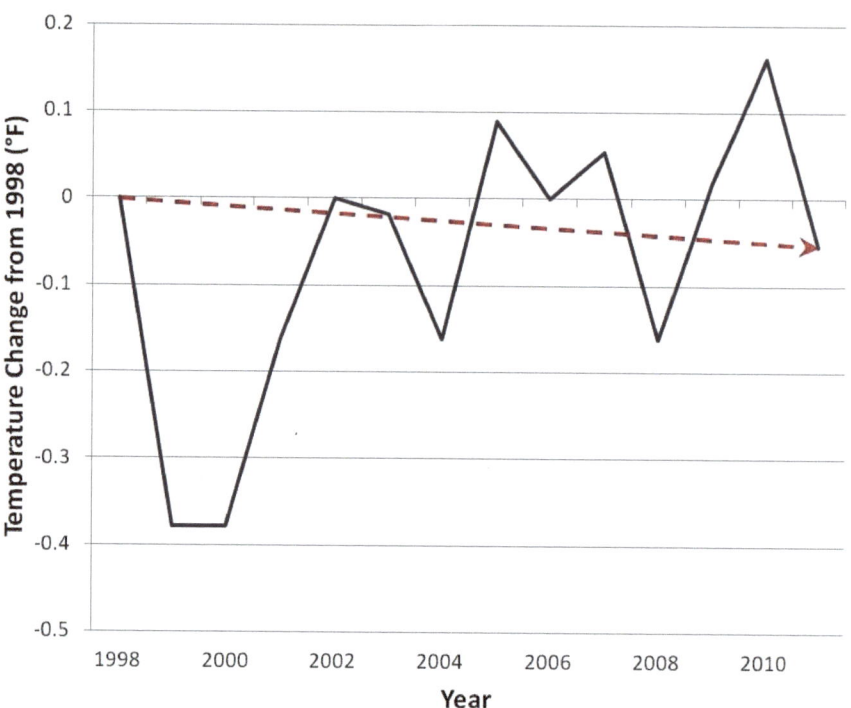

As we can see from visualising all the data though, the gradual incline of the slope from 1880 to 2014 shows that there is a clear case in favour of the theory of global warming.

Omit the y-axis labels

Back in 2013, the CEO of Apple, Tim Cook, made a live presentation to show how sales of the new iPhone had taken off. I wasn't there (I guess my invitation got lost in the post), but I have seen some photos of the event. One of them really stood out, but for all the wrong reasons. Monsieur Cook had put the following graph up on the screen to illustrate his point:

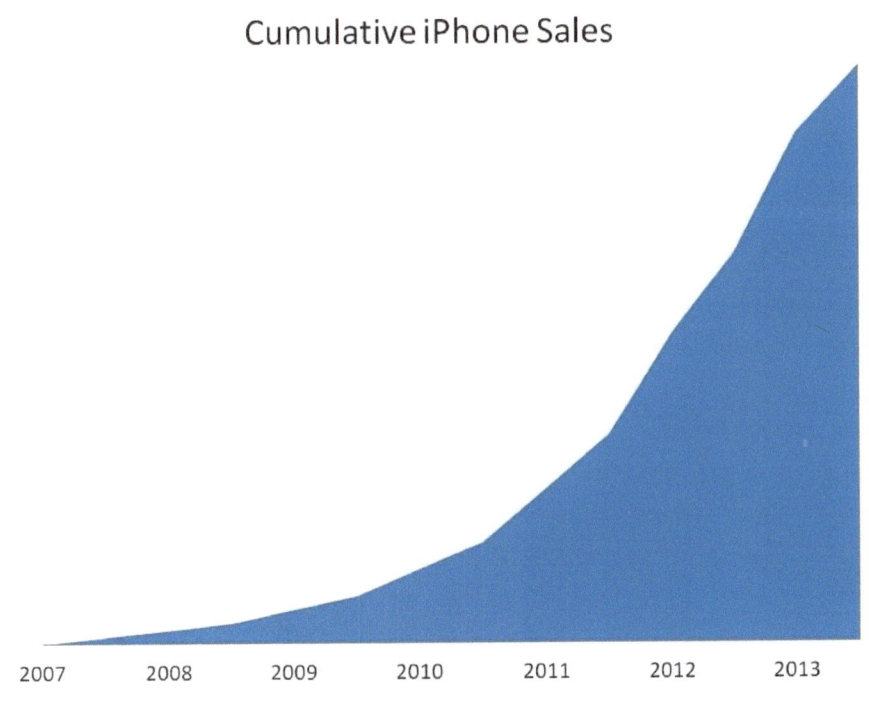

To be clear, I haven't had access to the actual data that sits behind this graph (and I bet that only a few select people in the world have), but I made measurements of each plot point with a ruler, and then recreated the graph. It's a pretty accurate representation of the actual graph that he showed, even if I do say so myself!

The point is that the graph keeps going up as you move your eyes from left to right. Sales are increasing! Or are they? Notice that there is the word 'Cumulative' in the header. That's the first clue that all is not well. If sales had indeed continued to increase year on year he would have shown it! If he's showing us cumulative sales, then he's trying to hide something. The second clue, and is meant to deceive (sorry Mr Cook, but it is, isn't it?), is that he deliberately omitted the y-axis. How many sales were there? No idea! There could have been billions of iPhone sales or there could have been hundreds. What is clear is that if there had been a lot of them, we'd have known about it. I inferred from this graph that not only have there not been as many iPhone sales as they were expecting, but that sales weren't progressing so well.

Let's deconstruct the data and see what the graph of Actual iPhone Sales looks like (see graph overleaf).

Whilst it appears to be the case that iPhone sales experienced strong growth in the earlier years, after 2012 sales seemed to drop off in some periods. In particular, the final bar on the graph is significantly shorter than each of the previous three. Is that a cause for concern for Apple's CEO? I'm not suggesting that these *aren't* healthy growth figures, but clearly, Tim Cook wasn't entirely happy with them, otherwise he would have just given it to us straight. Perhaps the total number of sales was the reason for the deception in his graph, but we will never know – the y-axis was omitted, so he could have us believe anything he wanted!

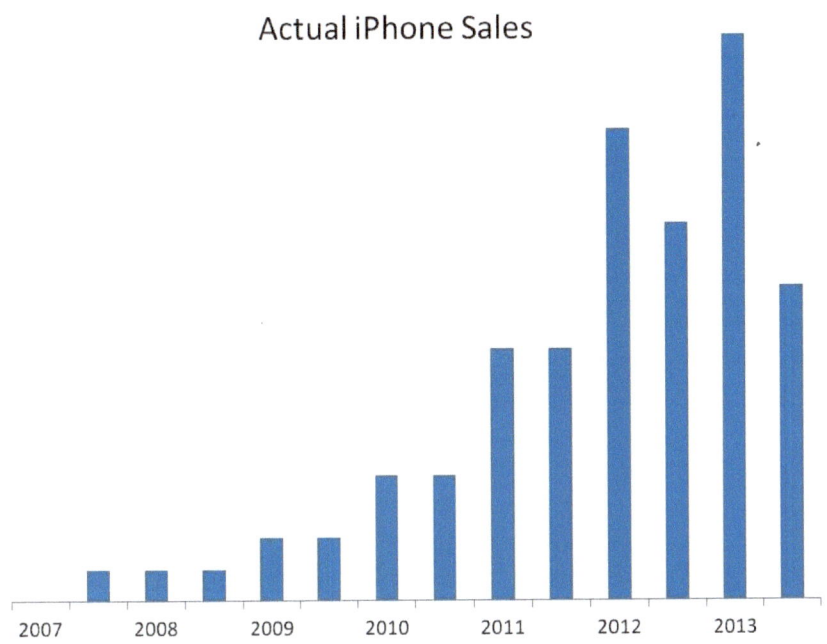

Extrapolate

Jim Hines was the first man to break the 10-second barrier for the 100 metres sprint in a time of 9.95 seconds at the Mexico Olympics on 14th October 1968. In a remarkable race, dubbed the Night of Speed, Ronny Ray Smith and Charles Greene (the previous world record holder from the night before) also ran under 10 seconds. It was to be another 15 years before the world record time was beaten again, but in a golden age of men's sprinting the record was bettered eight times (excluding drug-assisted times) in a 12 year period from 1987 to 1999. Then came Usain Bolt, who made all previous records look like they were set whilst running into a hurricane strength headwind. Oh my!

Overleaf is a graph of all the world records in the men's 100m since Jim Hines first broke the 10-second barrier.

If you had plotted these data in 1990 and looked at the graph, you would see that the plot points fall on a straight line. Extrapolating (extending into the future), you would be able to predict the progression of the world record times for the 1990s, the 2000s and 2010s. If you did that, you would see the line labelled '1' on the graph, which predicts that the 9.9-second barrier would be broken around 2010-ish. If you'd rushed off to the bookmaker's to put your shirt on it being broken in 2010 you would have been disappointed – the 9.9 second barrier was broken as early as 1991 by Carl Lewis.

This is the problem with extrapolating. It assumes that the pattern that was observed in the past will continue into the future. If there is one thing that I can guarantee in this life, it is that change is inevitable. And taxes. Change and taxes. Two things, two things I can guarantee – change and taxes. And death. Three things can I guarantee…

Oh dear, I seem to have lost myself in a Monty Python sketch… I'll come in again.

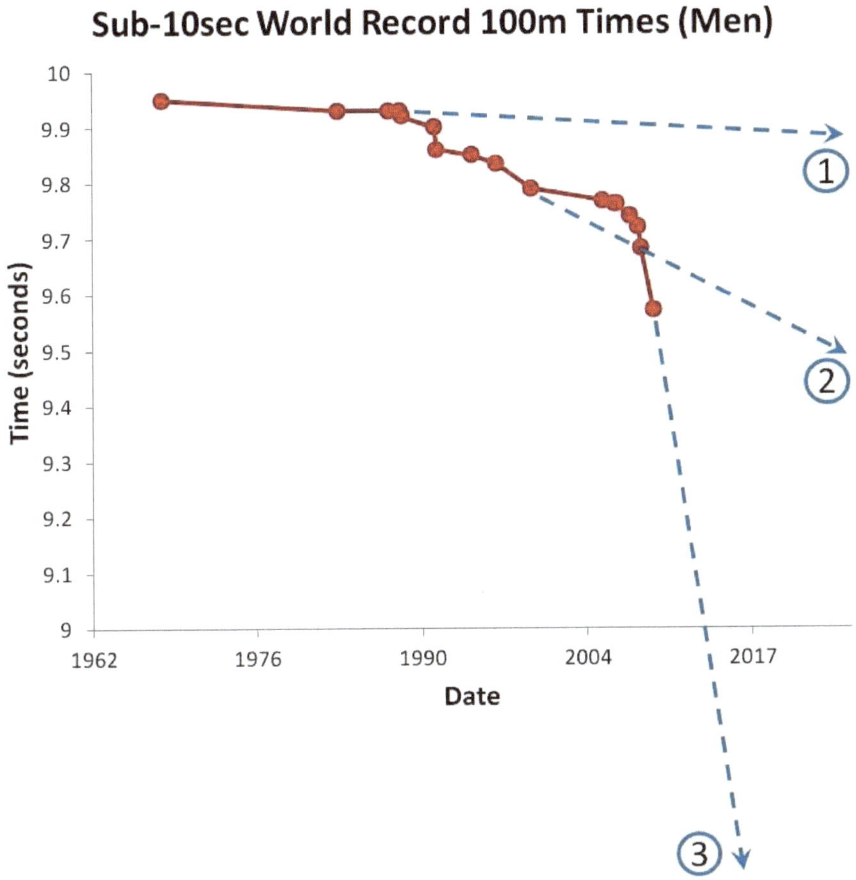

If, on the other hand, you were to consider only the golden age between 1987 and 1999 and extrapolate from there, you would get the line labelled '2'. Notice how very few of the plot points beyond 1999 actually lie on the extrapolation line... Finally, extrapolate the world record times from the Usain Bolt era and see what happens. The first person to break through the 9.0-second barrier will do so in 2010. Quick, get down to the bookies and... Oh, wait, we can't – it's already 2017 and the world record still stands at only 9.572 seconds.

We can continue doing ridiculous things like this and extrapolate line 3 even further to predict that eventually the 0.0-second barrier will be breached and the winner of the race will pass the finish line before the starting gun has been fired.

Here is what Mark Twain had to say on the subject of extrapolation:

"In the space of 176 years the Lower Mississippi has shortened itself 242 miles. That is an average of a trifle over one mile and a third per year. Therefore, any calm person, who is not blind or idiotic, can see that in the Old Oolitic Silurian Period, just a million years ago next November, the Lower Mississippi River was upwards of one million three hundred thousand miles long, and stuck out over the Gulf of Mexico like a fishing-rod. And by the same token any person can see that 742 years from now the Lower Mississippi will be only a mile and three quarters long, and Cairo and New Orleans will have joined their streets together, and be plodding comfortably along under a single mayor and a mutual board of aldermen. There is something fascinating about science. One gets such wholesale returns of conjecture out of such a trifling investment of fact."

And this very trick is commonplace to the statistical conman – in 1995, this remarkable statistic was quoted in a reputable journal:

"Every year since 1950, the number of children gunned down has doubled".

Do you want to do the maths on this or shall I?

If we start out with a single death in 1950, there will be two deaths in 1951, four in 1952, 1,024 in 1960 and over a million in 1970. We are nowhere near 1995 yet, and already the numbers are looking scary. Let's keep going. In 1980 there will be a billion children gunned down, a trillion in 1990, 35 trillion in 1995 – the year the quote was published – and a billion trillion squadrillion by 2000. Oh my, it seems the human propensity to gun down children has spread far beyond the Earth and has now infected the rest of the Galaxy. Where do we go from here and what should we do next? Get more children or fewer guns, perhaps?

Pie Charts

In Cockney rhyming slang, 'Pork Pies' means Lies. That's quite insightful, as it happens, because pie charts are one of the easiest ways of telling 'porkies', or lies. There are many ways of manipulating pie charts to make the data appear a certain way, but even with just a simple non-adulterated pie chart it can be difficult to understand what the data are trying to tell you.

Take a look at the following pie chart of the top 10 leading causes of death globally between 2000 and 2015, according to the World Health Organisation:

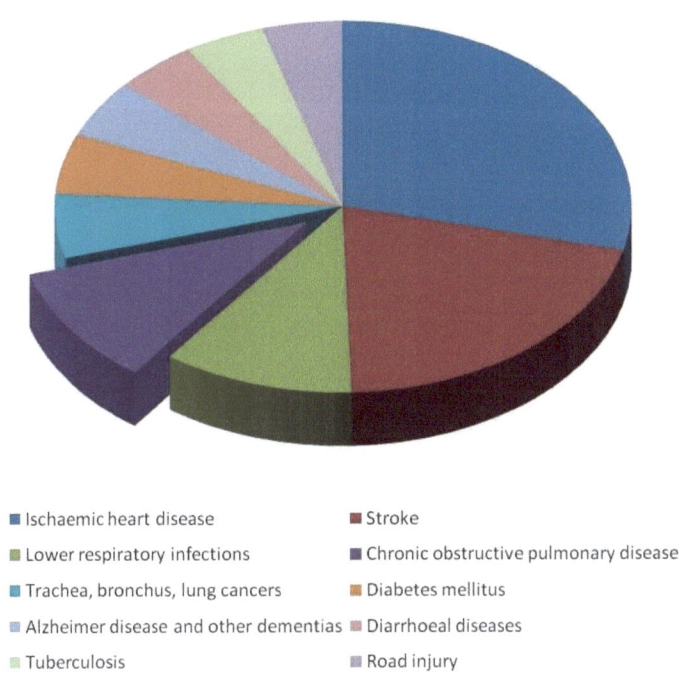

- Ischaemic heart disease
- Stroke
- Lower respiratory infections
- Chronic obstructive pulmonary disease
- Trachea, bronchus, lung cancers
- Diabetes mellitus
- Alzheimer disease and other dementias
- Diarrhoeal diseases
- Tuberculosis
- Road injury

Just trying to figure out which labels correspond to the chunks of the graph is difficult, but let's take Chronic obstructive pulmonary disease (COPD) – the purple cut-out chunk (South West on the pie chart). What proportion of the whole is COPD? To my eyes, it's about 1/3 of a right angle, so about 30°. Out of 360°, that makes 1/12 of the whole or about 8.3%. How well did I do? The actual figure is 5.6%, so my estimate was too large by half.

The margins for error when making measurements and calculations of pie charts are typically quite large, which is why pie charts are used by the unscrupulous!

Comparisons are difficult to make too. Compare COPD to Trachea, bronchus and lung cancers (TBLC) – the light purple chunk located between 11 and 12 o' clock. If you wanted to compare the differences in size between these, it is difficult to make your eyes ignore the depth of the COPD section. The TBLC section of the graph has no depth, so a direct comparison can be misleading. Is COPD about 3 times the size of TBLC? Actually, it's less than twice the size.

A wonderful example of how not to present data in a pie chart came courtesy of Fox News during the 2012 primaries. The news anchor, Bryon Harlan, presented a pie chart showing the support enjoyed by Sarah Palin, compared to that of her opponents Mike Huckabee and Mitt Romney (overleaf).

The areas of the three chunks suggest that each of the candidates has roughly equal support, until you look at the percentage share of the support that each of the candidates received – Sarah Palin has 10% more support than Mitt Romney. But wait, there's more. Add up the percentages and you get 193%. What? What does that mean? Well, to get an answer to that we're going to have to dig around in the original data. It turns out that this was a telephone poll that asked 900 registered voters if they had a favourable or unfavourable opinion of a list of names. The numbers reported on the graph are the favourability ratings among voters who identified themselves as Republicans. Notice that the question in the poll ('favourability' – rate each on the list) was very different from the one reported on Fox News ('support' – choose one Republican candidate).

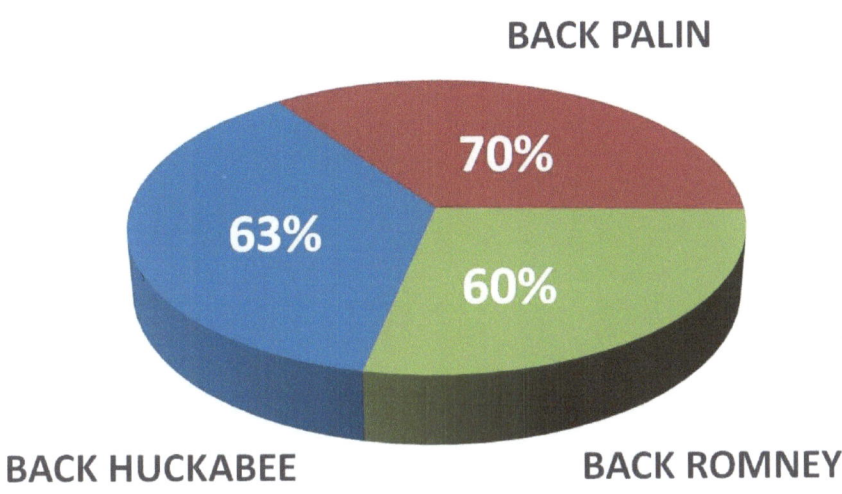

Interestingly, the original data also showed that Newt Gingrich scored 58% on the poll, just 2% behind Mitt Romney, but for some reason they decided to leave him off altogether. Baffling. Perhaps they thought it stretched credulity for the slices of the pie chart to add up to 251% rather than 193%. I guess we'll never know.

Even more interesting was that Oprah Winfrey, who wasn't a politician and wasn't running in the primaries, had a 46% favourability rating from Republican voters and an 80% rating from Democrat voters – the highest favourability rating in the entire poll.

So what can we read into these data? Pretty much nothing. Who is going to win the election? I haven't a clue, but my money is on Oprah!

Here is one of my favourite pie charts, showing the exit poll from the 2017 UK General Election, as printed widely by The Sun newspaper (and faithfully reproduced by my fair hand):

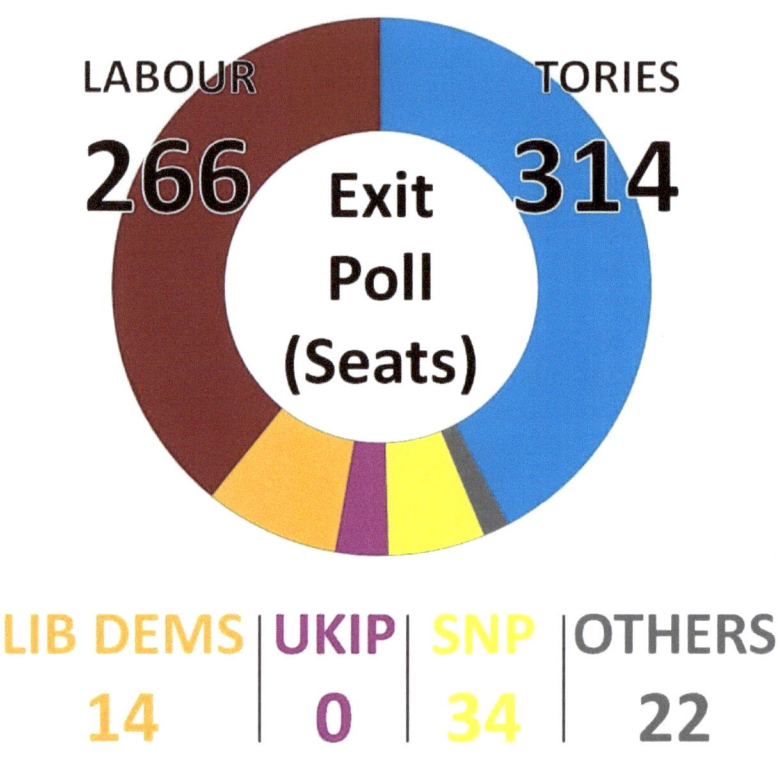

Nothing amiss here, is there? Well, nothing obvious, at least until you start to look and compare the numbers. Take a closer look and see if you can spot what is going on.

Did you notice that UKIP got no seats in the election, but they have a spot on the pie chart? Did you also notice that UKIP has a larger slice of the pie than Others, who got 22 seats?

I can imagine some kind of comedy sketch going on with these numbers, like:

"Is 34 a bigger number than 14, or is it smaller?"

"Oh, smaller, it's definitely smaller…"

"What about zero then?"

"Well, zero is a bit less than 34 but it's much more than 22…"

3D Charts

Perhaps the best way to mislead your audience with legitimate graphs is by plotting your data on 3D axes and then playing around with the various options available to you. For example, suppose that your research organisation spends far too much on administration, and although you need to report it truthfully, there is nothing to stop you reporting it unfairly. Take a look at the stacked bar chart on the left:

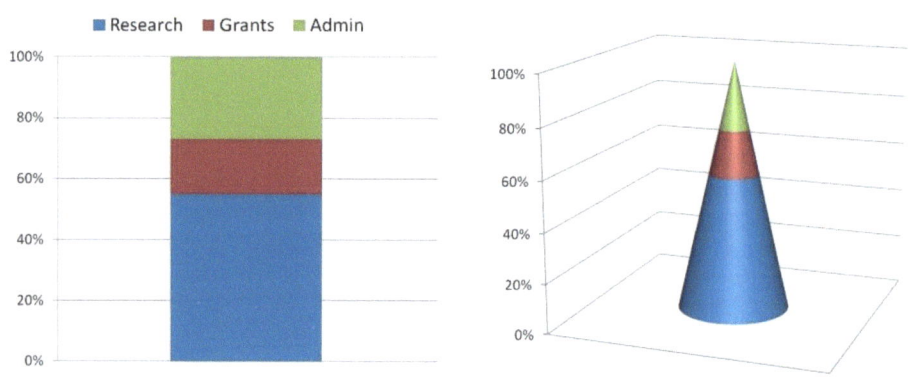

This is a fair and correct way to report that your administration costs are 27% of the total expenditure. On the other hand, 27% is quite a large chunk of all the costs and might raise questions about just what the hell you're spending it on. You need to report it correctly but make it *appear* smaller – enter the stacked cone plot on the right. With this, the correct way to read it is to take into account only the vertical height of each section. Yeah, but who does that when you have all that 3D loveliness? Of course you're going to look at the whole volume of the cone – that's why it's there! Can you really tell from the cone plot that administration costs are 50% larger than grant costs? It looks the other way around to me...

Another favoured 3D tool to play around with is perspective. Hold a toy cow between your fingers and then look at it while simultaneously looking out of the window at the real cow in yonder field. They look the same size, don't they? And yet you know that the one *out there* is waaayyy bigger than the one *in here*. That's the power of perspective – it can make even tiny things look bigger than big things. And you can use it to do the same tricks with your graphs.

Let's have another look at a couple of graphs that we've seen before and see what we can do with these when we sprinkle a little perspective pixie dust magic into the mix. Remember Tim Cook's graph about iPhone sales? Well I've re-plotted it as a 3D graph with some added perspective (below left), and voila – the slope appears much steeper suggesting a faster rate of growth, and it's also harder to spot that sales are slowing in the latter couple of years. Moreover, it would have been much harder for me to have measured the heights at each plot point to re-construct his 'real' chart!

And what about the exit polls at the 2017 election? What if I had wanted to show that the Tories won by a landslide (which they didn't – they had a minority of seats and ended up in a coalition with the DUP)? There is nothing wrong with the original pie chart that a little perspective cannot fix – see the pie chart above right. Not only have I changed the chart from 2D to 3D and altered the perspective, but I've also changed the sizes of the text labels to accentuate 'Tories' over 'Labour'. In reality, the Tories won only 48% of Parliamentary seats, but on my super-duper 3D chart, it looks like they won about 60% of them. Pixie dust magic indeed!

Pictocharts

Let's face it, graphs are boring. Sorry, but they are. Whether they are line charts, histograms, time series or scatter plots, they are all somehow designed to put us to sleep. Sure, they might contain some useful information and they can be used to convey some really important facts (or untruths, as we've seen), but really, do they have to be so dull and depressing?

Well actually, no, they don't – we can jazz them up with pretty pictures, and yet still tell the same story.

Welcome to the wonderful world of the pictochart!

Whenever you see a bar chart, simply exchange the bars for colourful pictures of fruit, cows, stacks of coins, houses – in fact, anything your heart desires. All we need to do is make sure that the heights of the images match the heights of the bars we're replacing and taa-daa – instant appeal.

And they don't lie. Oh no, not pictocharts. They might give the *impression* of a different story, but interpretation is in the eye of the beholder.

Let's take an example in which we compare the average monthly wage of men in the US and the UK. Typically, we might plot these as a bar chart with, as usual, correctly labelled axes, like the one on the left overleaf:

Perfectly fine graph, you might say. All correct and proper, if a little boring and stiff. To make it altogether more exciting we could take out the bars and replace them with bags of cash, like the pictochart above right. Ah, that's better. And the information is still correct, isn't it? After all, the height of the UK wage is $2000 across both charts, and similarly $4000 for the US wage.

Yes indeed, but does the US bag of cash *look* like it is twice the size of the UK bag? Certainly not! It looks like you could get four UK bags inside one US bag, so while the bar chart image tells us that the US wage is twice that in the UK, the pictorial image conveys the message that the US wage is four times that in the UK.

Well, that is, of course, if you are assessing the area of the bags of cash. If instead you consider that the bags are three dimensional, then you'll be making a volume assessment. Then you could fit eight UK bags inside a single US bag.

This is how pictocharts are extremely misleading; persuading us that 2 x 2 does not make 4, but instead makes 8, or perhaps even 16 – and all without telling a lie!

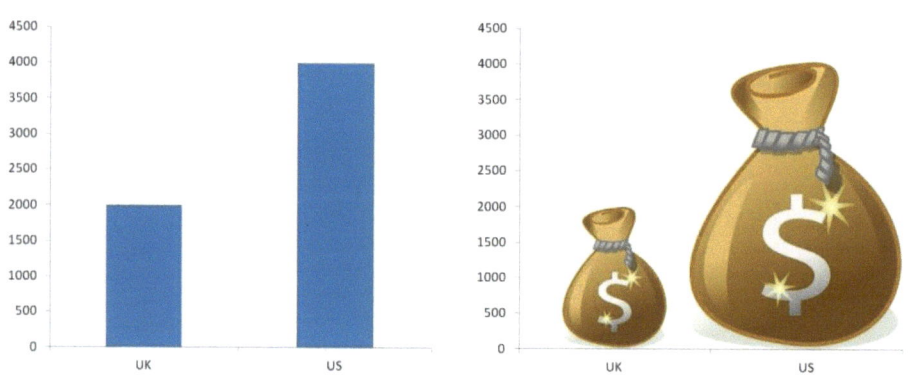

So changing the area or volumes of the image elements can make a big impact on the perception of the information contained within the data. Similarly, the image itself can shed a little shade where it ought not to. For example, let us say we wish to show the nutritional content of various fruit, or their natural sugar content or their price, or whatever. Instead of a boring histogram, we could use images of the fruit themselves as bar charts, like the one on the next page.

Clearly, three bananas are equal to three pears, and both are more than two apples. Or are we talking about bunches of bananas and pairs of pears? And did you notice how three pears are taller than three bananas? Was that intentional or are they supposed to be the same height? Now if I tell you that, buried within the text in the small print on an entirely different page, one banana represents 3000 tonnes of bananas, one apple is equal to 5000 tonnes of apples and one pear equals 2000 tonnes of pears, what would the graph now tell us? Absolutely nothing! The heights of the bar chart can't be read off the y-axis because it doesn't exist, so how could we possibly compare them? Apparently, we are meant to understand that 9000 tonnes of bananas and 6000 tonnes of pears are more than 10,000 tonnes of apples. The mind boggles!

Oh, the lies we can tell when using images instead of graphs…

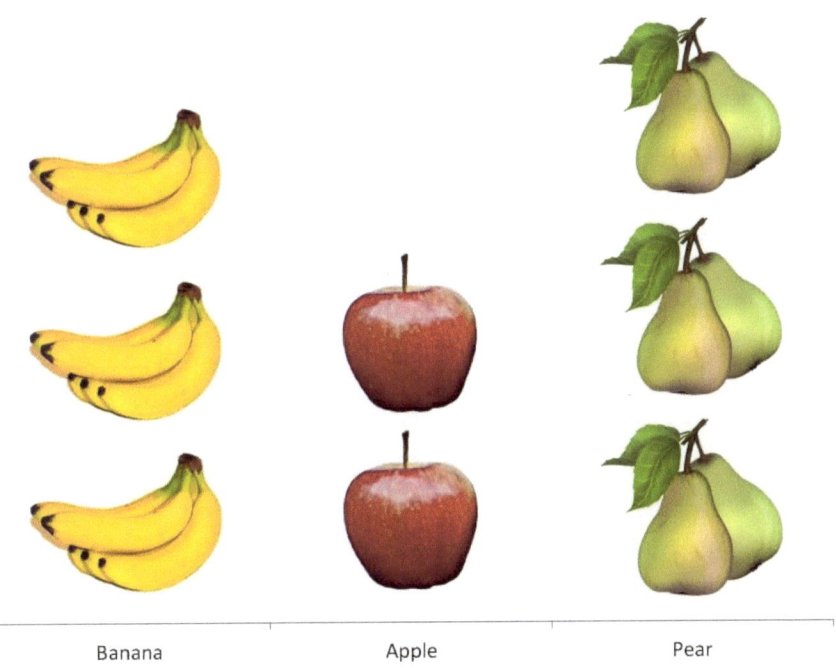

Like how we can show that the decline in the population of African elephants isn't really a cause for alarm at all. We can simply show an image of an elephant to show elephant numbers in 1950 alongside a smaller image to represent the numbers in 2000, like this:

Sure, the numbers of elephants has declined, but the decline isn't so big is it? I mean, it just looks like a baby elephant with a mummy elephant. How cute! Surely, the creators of the image (the political wing of the Royal Society of International African Elephant Poachers) would be truthful and not actually misrepresent the data by fudging the sizes of the images wouldn't they?

Well, the African elephant population in the 1930s and 1940s was estimated to be around 3-5 million, and in 2014 the population was estimated to be around 700,000. Conservatively, that means that the elephant population has declined to one-quarter of its size (or worse). Reading the heights of the images (as we are supposed to do with graphs) tells us that the 2000 population is around half of that in 1950. So the graph lied then? Not quite. You see, the *areas* of the elephants are in the proportion of 4:1, so the pictograph tells the truth (ish), as long as you read the areas and not the heights. Omitting all axes from the pictograph means that the reader can interpret the image in *any way they wish*, and it is not the fault of the image creator if the reader gets it wrong...

Epilogue

When it comes to lying, there is no better way than to do it with graphs. There is something compelling about the way they are presented, the way that the 'facts' wash over you and bore into your consciousness without you being burdened by any of the tiresome details. It is easy to be seduced. Want to accentuate certain features? That's fine; you will probably fool most of the audience who won't take the time to look more closely. Would you like to sell more product or get more votes, but the numbers betray you? No problem, just grab the numbers that you wish to present (truthful or otherwise) and present them on a graph that shows your version of the 'truth' in the best light possible.

Now you know how it is done by the political conmen. When truncating axes and omitting axis labels you can distort reality to such a degree that you can make people believe that the earth is flat (yes, some still believe this) or that global warming is a fallacy (there are a *lot* of people that believe this). With extrapolation, you can convince your audience of anything you like. Any pair of numbers can be used with this trick and any trend can be up, down or in any direction that pleases you. Other plot points might give the game away, so you might wish not to show them. Remember the abortion *versus* cancer plot from earlier? How many plot points from each were used? Just a single pair. And what about the graph used to 'prove' that the world is cooling rather than warming? How many plot points were used to convince? Again, just two. See how it's done? Simple, isn't it?

At times, bar charts, line charts and scatter plots are not on your side, and somehow you can't get the data to make your point very well. That's when the humble pie chart comes in. Pie charts are about the easiest way you can find to distort the truth or even tell outright lies – and get away with it. With pie charts you can bury data that you don't want to be seen, like in the pie chart that showed the support for Palin, Huckabee and Romney – Newt Gingrich was nowhere to be seen. Alternatively, you can accentuate, like in the pie chart from the Sun newspaper that gave a spot on the pie chart to UKIP, who didn't get a single seat in Parliament. Not only should UKIP not have had a spot on the chart, but they were even given a larger slice of the pie than Others, who won 22 seats. Incredible!

The best of the numerical charts to deceive, though, has to go to 3D charts – especially the 3D pie chart. We saw how we could turn 48% of votes into what looks like 60% in the case of the 2017 UK General Election. The numbers on the pie chart were truthful (at least, for the Tories and Labour), but changing the perspective made it look very different indeed.

The gold medal for graphic deception, though, simply has to go to the pictochart. With these, you don't even need numbers. Just display a pair of differently sized pretty pictures next to each other and you can leave the rest to the viewer's imagination. As we have seen, we can make 2x2 equal 8 or even 16 without breaking into a sweat. The heights of the adjacent images may be in the ratio 1:2, but what is seen – the areas and volumes – tells a different story. It's not even your fault if the reader misunderstands it, and this is your advantage.

So now you know how to lie with graphs. Graphs themselves don't lie, they are simply a representation of the data, and it is up to you how you represent those data. Be careful though, we are just beginning a new age in the evolution of mankind – the age of data – and we are all becoming ever more aware of your con tricks.

We are watching…

###

About The Author

Lee Baker is an award-winning software creator that lives behind a keyboard in a darkened room. Illuminated only by the light from his monitor, he aspires to finding the light switch.

With decades of experience in science, statistics and artificial intelligence, he has a passion for telling stories with data. Despite explaining it a dozen times, his mother still doesn't understand what he does for a living.

Insisting that data analysis is much simpler than we think it is, he authors friendly, easy-to-understand books that teach the fundamentals of data analysis and statistics.

His mission is to unleash your inner data ninja!

As the CEO of Chi-Squared Innovations, one day he'd like to retire to do something simpler, like crocodile wrestling.

Claim Your FREE eBook Now!

This is the sister book to **Graphs Don't Lie**, and teaches you how to lie with statistics

(if you're unscrupulous enough...)

Download your FREE copy right here:

https://chi2innovations.lpages.co/ebook-truth-lies-and-statistics/

Leave a Review

Thank you for reading **Graphs Don't Lie**.

I hope you enjoyed reading it as much as I enjoyed writing it. If you did, please take a moment to return to where you purchased this book and leave a review.

Thank you!

Lee Baker

www.ingramcontent.com/pod-product-compliance
Lightning Source LLC
Chambersburg PA
CBHW040339220526
45473CB00009B/2740